My BUTTERFLY BOUQUET

Written by

Nicola Davies

Illustrated by

Hannah Peck

wren & rook

When I came out of hospital, it was **winter**.

There were **no flowers**
in the garden, **no colours**.

Dad said, "I'll take you where we can find a bunch of colours. A whole **bouquet** of them!"

Dad's bouquet was inside a big glasshouse
where the air was warm and steamy.

It shimmered with bright colours –
swirls and spots and stripes.

Looking closer, I could see eyes
and legs and antennae. And
lots and lots of wings ...

Butterflies!

They dipped and danced in all directions
so you couldn't tell where they'd go next!

"It makes them difficult to catch," said Dad. "There are lots of things that like to **eat** a butterfly."

When they landed, they were
hard to see. Their folded wings
looked just like leaves or bark.

But some had spots that looked
like **eyes** and made me **jump**.

"I bet that would **scare**
a hungry bird away!" Dad laughed.

Some butterflies stood out even
when their wings were folded.

"Wouldn't those get eaten up?"
I asked.

"They've got a different trick!" Dad said.
"They're **poisonous** and their bright colour
is a warning that means 'don't eat me'!"

Butterflies were **everywhere** ...

They **fluttered** round the flowers and feeders, unrolling their long tongues like straws to suck up sweet nectar.

One landed on my hand and walked about. **It tickled!**

"Its **feet** are tasting you," Dad said, "to see if you're good to eat or if you're the sort of leaf where it could lay its eggs."

Of course, I tasted wrong so it flew off!

We searched for eggs.
They were really hard to find.

Some were all alone

and some in little clusters.

Each kind of butterfly had laid
its eggs on a different sort of plant.

"So when the tiny caterpillars hatch,
they have their favourite food to eat."

We found some caterpillars too!

We watched for ages
but **all** they did was eat.

"Eating is their job," said Dad,
"eating and growing." Some of
them were **massive!**

One really big one was wrapping itself up in fine white threads to make a little silken sac.

"It's making a chrysalis," said Dad, "so it can change into a butterfly."

I didn't see how something like a
caterpillar could grow wings and fly.

But Dad explained that inside the chrysalis,
the caterpillar's body breaks into tiny pieces
and then re-forms –

like a LEGO house broken
into all its bricks and rebuilt
to make a palace!

A butterfly began to crawl out of its chrysalis.
It looked all **wet** and **crumpled** but slowly
its wings stretched out.

They began to **shimmer** and we watched it fly away!

Outside the sky was grey and dull and I felt ill again. "It's weeks to go till spring!" I grumbled.

But Dad just **smiled** and said, "That gives us lots of time to get our garden ready!"

Around the edges of the garden we left the weeds
to grow, to give caterpillars food to eat.

Then we chose plants that would make
flowers with lots of nectar.

"A feast for butterflies!" Dad said.

Planting them was hard work, but
I was getting **stronger** every day.

At last spring came...
And one sunny afternoon, a butterfly arrived.

And then another.

Then three more ...

It's summer now and Dad says that I am
blooming like a flower and growing like a weed!

Every day we sit together in the garden,
in the middle of our very own ...

BOUQUET OF

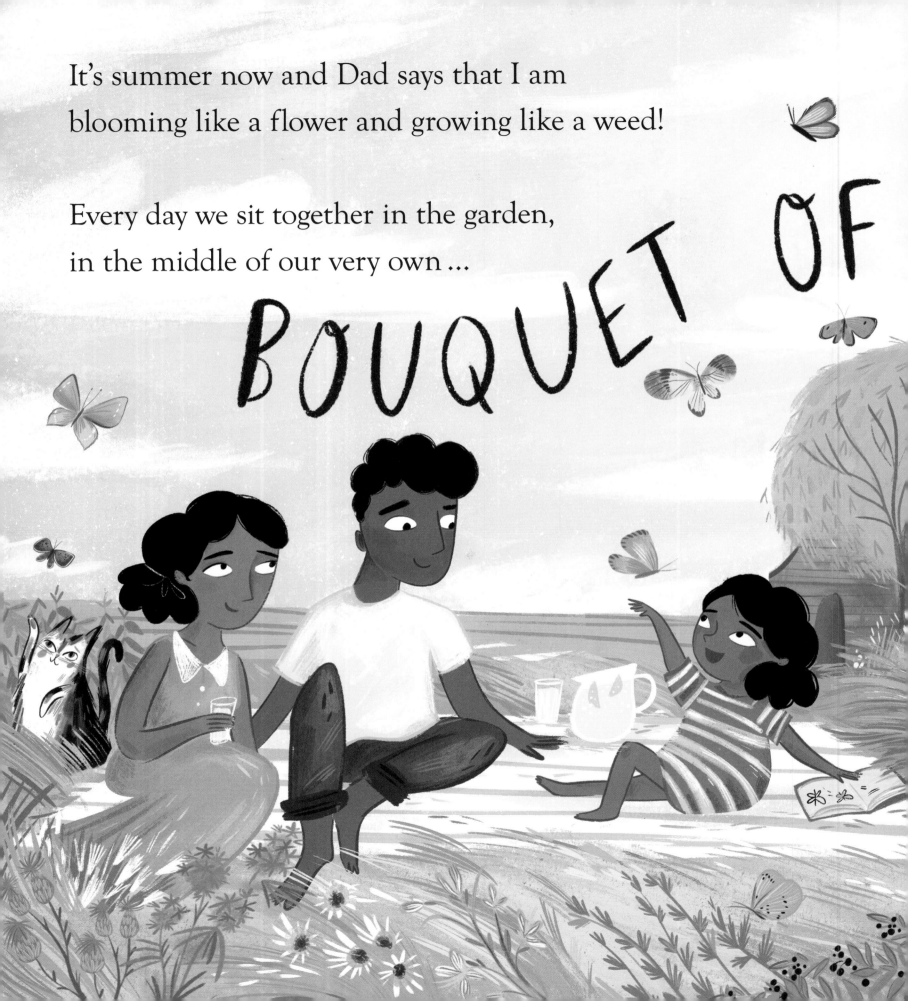

BUTTERFLIES

FLOWERS NEED BUTTERFLIES and BUTTERFLIES NEED FLOWERS!

Animals need a male and a female to make babies, and flowers do too. Pollen from the male part of a flower, the stamen, must get to the female part, the stigma, of another flower to make seeds. Plants can't walk so they get insects to do the work of carrying pollen for them.

They tempt the insects with the bright colours, scents and sweet nectar of their flowers. While the insects are sipping on the nectar, they get dusted with pollen, which they then carry away to another flower. This is called pollination, and the animals that do it, like bees and butterflies, are called pollinators.

Many foods we like to eat, such as apples, strawberries, peaches, cherries, tomatoes and courgettes, and nearly all our wildflowers, would disappear without insect pollinators. We need butterflies, bees and other insects to help us grow food and keep our countryside beautiful.

Bees and butterflies work in different ways. Bees will visit every flower in a small area, but butterflies travel further between flowers. So they bring pollen from a greater distance, from flowers that may be just a little bit different; this helps to create a variety of strong, healthy seeds and fruits.

Humans have made life tough for butterflies and other pollinators. Our towns and cities leave little green space for them, our pesticides kill them and climate change is making it harder for them to survive.

But there are a few simple things you can do to help and protect butterflies:

- Plant flowers to give butterflies nectar to feed on from spring right through to autumn (even a pot planted with the right flowers will do). *Verbena bonariensis*, oregano, marigolds and buddleia are all good for providing butterflies with nectar.

- Leave patches of grass and nettles to grow tall, and plant nasturtiums to give caterpillars some of their favourite foods.

- Never use pesticides.

You can download this free leaflet to tell you more: http://tinyurl.com/butterflyleaflet

MARIGOLD

EGGS

A butterfly's life begins as an egg, tiny as a pinhead, sitting on a leaf alone or with lots of others. The mother butterfly who laid the egg chose the leaf very carefully so that it would be the right sort for her caterpillars to eat when they hatch. But before they can tuck into the leaf, they must eat their egg case!

CATERPILLARS

A caterpillar's body is just a tube with jaws for biting and a mouth for chewing, three pairs of little legs at the front and five pairs of legs at the back. It can smell with its tiny antennae and see light and dark with twelve simple eyes. A caterpillar only needs to eat and grow, so a basic body like this works fine.

As caterpillars grow, their skin gets too tight, so they have to wriggle out of it. They swallow air to stretch the new skin underneath, so it can have room to grow even more.

A caterpillar may shed its skin six times, and grow to be 1000 times heavier than it was when it hatched, before it is ready for the next stage of its life.

BUTTERFLY

ADULT

After as little as ten days, or as long as months or even years, the chrysalis splits open and the new adult butterfly crawls out. It has six long legs, antennae, big eyes and two pairs of wings: everything it needs to fly around and find a mate, flowers to feed from, and a place to lay eggs, starting the next generation of butterflies.

LIFE CYCLE

PUPA

When it's grown enough, the caterpillar stops eating and crawls away somewhere safe. It uses the silk glands on its head to weave a coat around its body. Under this coat, its skin changes to form a shell. Inside this chrysalis, or pupa, the caterpillar's simple body transforms completely into the body of an adult butterfly, a process called metamorphosis.

Both caterpillars and butterflies have clever ways to protect themselves from predators:

- Patterns and colouring that help camouflage them so they blend in with their environment
- Bright, startling eyespots to scare away potential enemies
- Poisons in their bodies and vivid warning colours that signal they are dangerous to eat.

For Alice, Henry, Elsie-Rose, Emma, Lucy,
Wilf, Flora, Hespa and Nettie with love – N.D.

For Tom – H.P.

First published in Great Britain in 2020
by Wren & Rook

Text copyright © Nicola Davies, 2020
Illustration copyright © Hannah Peck, 2020
Design copyright © Hodder & Stoughton Ltd, 2020
All rights reserved.

The right of Nicola Davies and Hannah Peck to be
identified as the author and illustrator respectively of
this Work has been asserted by them in accordance with
the Copyright, Designs & Patents Act 1988.

HB ISBN: 978 1 5263 6129 5
PB ISBN: 978 1 5263 6131 8
E-book ISBN: 978 1 5263 6130 1
10 9 8 7 6 5 4 3 2 1

Wren & Rook
An imprint of Hachette Children's Group
Part of Hodder & Stoughton
Carmelite House
50 Victoria Embankment
London EC4Y 0DZ

An Hachette UK Company
www.hachette.co.uk
www.hachettechildrens.co.uk

Publishing Director: Debbie Foy
Senior Editors: Alice Horrocks and Liza Miller
Art Director: Laura Hambleton
Designer: Barbara Ward

Printed in China

LEGO ® is a registered trade mark of
LEGO Juris A/S.

MIX
Paper from
responsible sources
FSC
www.fsc.org   FSC® C104740